Athlone in Old Photographs

Gearóid O'Brien

GILL & MACMILLAN

405556

Gill & Macmillan Ltd
Hume Avenue
Park West
Dublin 12
with associated companies throughout the world
www.gillmacmillan.ie

© 2002 Gearóid O'Brien
0 7171 3471 7
Design and print origination by O'K Graphic Design, Dublin
Printed in Malaysia

A catalogue record is available for this book from the British Library.

1 3 5 4 2

Contents

Introduction

The name Athlone (in Irish Áth Luain) literally means 'The ford of Luan'. This ancient fording point on the middle Shannon has been of strategic importance since time immemorial. The town itself developed as an Anglo-Norman settlement around a castle built for King John by his Irish Justiciar. The castle was built on land belonging to the Cluniac priory of SS Peter & Paul which stood on the west bank of the Shannon.

Today Athlone is regarded as the Capital of the Irish Midlands and the Gateway to the West. In medieval times the town was situated on the boundaries of Meath and Connaught. Today, for administrative purposes, it lies in County Westmeath. The river Shannon still divides the town into two Catholic parishes and two dioceses: St Mary's, to the east, in Ardagh and Clonmacnois and St Peter's, to the west in Elphin. The suburban area west of Athlone belongs in County Roscommon and the province of Connaught while Athlone town belongs in County Westmeath and the province of Leinster.

A man-made causeway across the Shannon at Athlone existed since the year 1000 AD at least, while the earliest recorded bridge was built in 1120. The earliest bridges and castles at Athlone were of wicker and wooden construction and thus were short lived. The first stone castle was erected in 1210 while a permanent bridge was not constructed until Elizabethan times. The Cluniac order had their only Irish priory on the west bank of the Shannon at Athlone (from *circa* 1150) while the Franciscans built their monastery on the east bank (*circa* 1240).

From the mid-thirteenth century Athlone was a walled town. In Elizabethan times gatehouses were built to the east and in the 1650s (following their destruction during the Confederate Wars) a major renewal of the urban fortifications was carried out. The Connaught town was defended by a series of earthen fortifications while the town wall on the Leinster side was repaired and strengthened. However, these fortifications were to come under heavy fire during the famous sieges of Athlone in 1690 and 1691 and today only fragments survive.

The two sieges of Athlone were part of the infamous Williamite and Jacobite Wars in Ireland. In 1690 the then Governor of Athlone, Col Richard Grace, successfully defended the town against the might of a 10,000 strong Williamite force. In 1691 the Williamites returned to Athlone with a force of 25,000 men under the command of a Dutch General, Godard de Ginkle. Ironically they discovered the very ford that gave Athlone its name, and in a surprise attack, took the town and castle by storm. For his services to King William, Godard de Ginkle was created Earl of Athlone.

A series of Napoleonic fortifications to the west of Athlone has given rise to the modern place-name the Batteries. Following the outbreak of war with the French Republic and the attempted landing of the French at Bantry Bay a total of eight defensive batteries were constructed on the western perimeter of the town. All but a small portion of the No 1 Battery have been destroyed.

The nineteenth century witnessed several great milestones in the history and development of Athlone. The first of these was the Shannon navigation works of the 1840s which made the Shannon fully navigable at Athlone. Prior to this all major river traffic had been diverted through a canal which was constructed to the west of the town in 1757. By 1851 the first trains had crossed the railway bridge opening up a new era in public transport.

This nineteenth-century engraving shows the Northgate with the short-lived, man-made, Stirabout Harbour in the foreground. To the left of the gatehouse the old bell-tower of St Mary's complete with steeple can be seen, while to the right is the tower of the Tholsel or Market House. The Northgate stood at the junction of Northgate Street and the present St Francis Terrace. It was demolished around 1840. Stirabout Harbour (constructed circa 1822) disappeared with the Shannon navigation works of the 1840s.

The industrial development of Athlone received a major boost in 1859 with the opening of Athlone Woollen Mills. The founder, Dr Edward M. Gleeson, in partnership with William Smith, built up an industry which acquired a world-wide reputation for the quality of its tweed. At the height of its fame this factory was employing 500, making it the single largest employer in Athlone. Tragically the Mills were destroyed by fire on the night of 11 November 1940 and never regained their status as the major local employer. Fortunately in the late 1930s General Textiles (Gentex) had opened a new factory on the site of the Ranelagh School. Here among other products the famous 'Constellation Sheets' were made. Gentex continued to operate until 1984 and by that time Athlone had a diversity of smaller manufacturing industries ready to take up the slack. Today Athlone is surrounded by industrial estates where a number of major factories provide excellent employment opportunities to both local workers and suitably skilled and qualified personnel from Ireland and abroad.

A significant development in the life of the town was the setting up of the first photographers studio in Athlone around 1860. John T. Hoban was the earliest resident photographer, though we know that prior to that itinerant photographers had visited the town. Another nineteenth-century photographer who lived and worked in Athlone was James Macnee-Oliver. By the early twentieth century photography had become more widespread. The doyen of local photographers was G.V. Simmons (who was ably succeeded by his son J.O. Simmons and later by Roy Redpath). Another early exponent of the photographic art was Charlie Backhouse, an employee of Athlone Printing Works. By the mid century MacCormac Studios had been established with Jimmy and Dan MacCormack both producing fine studio and outdoor work; John Dolan had a studio in Main Street and by the late 1950s the *Westmeath Independent* had employed its first staff photographer. Among the photographers who have served the local press with distinction are: Michael Geoghegan, Angela Meares, Pat Waldron, P.J. Murray, John Casey, Paddy Devanney, Pádraic Devanney, Anne Hennessy and Joe Relihan. Athlone has also had some very talented amateur photographers including Dr Paul Chapman and Mr Tom Price. The most distinguished amateur is Mr Leo Mahon whose award-winning photographs have graced several exhibitions and enhanced a number of fine publications.

This volume in the *Images of Ireland* series attempts to record for posterity the changing face of Athlone and I feel very privileged to have been asked to compile it. I hope that the balance which I have provided will be of interest to all those who love this town as much as I do. My own interest in old photographs goes back over thirty years. I had as one of my earliest mentors the late Billy English, who was then in the process of building up a collection of old images of Athlone for the archives of the Old Athlone Society. I marvelled at his ability to interpret the evidence presented in each photograph and, based on his powers of observation, to hazard an educated guess at the vintage of any given photograph. Today I am doing this myself as a matter of course.

When I joined the staff of Athlone Library in the early 1970s I was delighted to discover that the then Librarian, Mr Ernan Morris, had a fine collection of old photographs on file in the Library. During the course of almost thirty years these two collections have merged and at present I am the proud custodian of both. In the interim I have received very generous donations of photographs from individuals and families. Over the years I have benefited from the shared wisdom of several older inhabitants, including the late Larry Hanley NT, Michael Graham, Frank Egan and Joe Dowling, who have helped to identify many faces of old Athlone. Others who have helped are happily alive and well, including Jimmy O'Connor and Syd Shine.

In presenting this collection I am conscious of our debt to the many fine photographers who have taken the trouble to record the changing face of our town. I hope this book will encourage others to preserve the present for the future and continue to donate material of interest to our local Photographic Collection.

Gearóid O'Brien

This engraving of Athlone Castle captures the atmosphere of the marketplace in the nineteenth century. The large gun defending the castle is possibly a depiction of the 'great gun of Athlone'. A famous Williamite toast goes as follows: 'To the glorious pious and immortal memory of the great and good King William, who freed us from Pope and Popery, knavery and slavery, brass money and wooden shoes, and he who refuses this toast may be damned, crammed and rammed down the great Gun of Athlone.'

Acknowledgments

In compiling this collection I was, happily, spoiled for choice. I was also very fortunate in having the co-operation and assistance of many photographers and private collectors – the photographers are mentioned by name in the introduction.

It would be impossible to thank everyone individually but I wish to express my deep gratitude to all those who helped in any way. To those who supplied individual photographs, who allowed the reproduction of copyright material, who assisted with the identification of people and places and who gave advice no matter how seemingly insignificant – my heartfelt thanks.

I would like to make special mention of several people who made my task easier: Ms Mary Farrell, County Librarian, Westmeath County Library; the staff of Athlone Public Library; The President & Council of the Old Athlone Society; Mrs Rosemary Furlong, Mr Dermod A. Foy, Mr Paddy Martin, Ms Katie McCay Duffy, Mr A.J. Faulkner, Mr Larry Fagan, Mr Joseph Mooney, Br Brian O'Halloran, Mrs Pauline Harrington, Mr Syd Shine, Mr Cieran Temple, Mr Cecil English, Mr James 'Sonny' Gallagher, and Ms Angela Hanley. Mr Ted Clifford of Midland Camera Shop, Athlone provided excellent care and attention with copying facilities for a number of old photographs.

I also wish to express my special thanks to Mrs Maureen Egan for her kind permission to quote from *Bridging the Gap: Athlone's Golden Mile 1920-1980* by Frank Egan. Written by a man who was gifted with a long life and a keen memory, this little book, which is sadly long out-of-print, was a major contribution to the social history of our town and is an indispensable source for anyone wanting to learn about old Athlone.

1

Around the Town

In this 1920s postcard we see a crowd assembled outside Athlone Post Office in Custume Place waiting to board the 'Magnet Bus' to Dublin. It is interesting to note that the Post Office is designated by its Irish title, 'Oifig an Phuist', while the street name plaques for Northgate Street are given in both Irish and English. Apart from the bus the preferred means of transport was clearly the tricycle, as there are two tricycles and one bicycle in the picture. The Post Office moved to its present location in 1937.

These three shop-fronts recall the glory that was Foy's in Church Street in the 1950s. The Foy family had held these prime premises since the 1920s — originally a bicycle and sports shop with a pawnbroker's next door run by Ned Foy. Later they were successfully run by brothers Jack and Ernest Foy, and as the signs above the door reveal there was little that Foy's didn't sell.

This view of Connaught Street is less than flattering and yet it is obvious that there were many small shops and pubs as well as private residences in this part of the street. As a child, in pre-decimal and pre-Euro times, I once had a puncture fixed (as a special concession) for the princely sum of one old ha'penny by Mr Kilmartin in Connaught Street. Over the years I had tried, and failed, to pinpoint the exact location of his bicycle repair shop until I spotted the crude sign above the gateway in this photograph: 'Kilmartin & Sons Cycle Dealers'.

This old building, in Garden Vale, was once the Catholic presbytery for St Mary's parish. It was probably built around 1795 when the Catholic chapel moved from Irishtown to Mardyke Street, and it served until 1862. It was later associated with the Geoghegan family who had a coach factory on the site of the old church, the site now occupied by the car-park for the Royal Hoey Hotel.

A gargantuan load in Mardyke Street. This picture recalls a time, perhaps forty years ago, when the car was not the only form of congestion on our main streets. It shows the aftermath of an auction, possibly in the Royal Hoey Hotel, with a precarious looking lorry load of soft-furnishings in the background, while a group of farmers chat to one another, seemingly oblivious to the wandering cow. Geoghegan's paper shop forms a backdrop to this busy scene.

The Prince of Wales Hotel as it looked in the late 1950s. A century earlier this had been Rourke's Hotel. In 1853 The Hon Martin Von Bruen (ex-president of the United States of America) stayed there. In 1861 it was acquired by John Bergin, who named it 'The Prince of Wales Hotel' in 1863. In the 1880s it passed into the hands of the Geoghegan family. Charles Stewart Parnell and the boxer John L. Sullivan were among a host of famous guests who stayed at 'The Prince'.

This photograph shows the ruins of the house in Castle Street in which T.P. O'Connor was born and in which his father once ran a billiard saloon. In *T.P.'s Weekly* in 1902 he wrote: ' ... at the top of the street where stands the house in which I was born and where I was again living, I saw a small crowd gathered around a man who was exciting much attention... he was well dressed, looking refined, seemed, indeed, to be that which he was called: "The Gentleman Organ Grinder" who for some mysterious reason was travelling all over Ireland.'

The 1990s witnessed one of the greatest eras of development in the history of Athlone. Fortunately local photographer P.J. Murray captured many of the changes on film. **Above** is a view looking up Pearse Street in December 1996 while **below** is a view looking down Pearse Street in February 1997; the buildings on the right hand side are the backs of houses in Connolly Street.

This early view of Victoria Place and Church Street may date to the 1880s and is certainly earlier than 1897. A pump which was installed in 1875 can just be seen on the right. The Post Office, run by the Stokes family, opened in Victoria Place in 1881 and had transferred across the street by 1897. The quaint-looking building adjoining the Post Office was the premises of Thomas Burgess & Sons, which was raised to the ground and rebuilt as a fine imposing edifice in 1899.

The Market Square, early twentieth century. The name above the door on the left is illegible but is most likely 'Farrell'. Next door, John Kennedy had a drapery store from at least 1898, until his retirement in 1924. The next premises was James Dixon & Sons until 1922, when it became Byrne O'Halloran & Co and later P.J. Byrne's, and the corner premises owned by D.E. Williams was The Palace Bar. Notice the main entrance gate to the Barracks off the Market Square.

A donkey is harnessed to an old horse-drawn hearse outside the Marist residence in Gleeson Street, after the auction of the contents of Geoghegan's Coach Yard in the 1950s.

Connaught Street was a relatively late arrival in the streetscape of Athlone. Unlike Church Street, where the merchant classes who moved into Athlone set up shop, this was very much an Irish street, closely connected with the farming families of south Roscommon. Some of those who formerly brought their produce to the market in Athlone set up business here in this street. In the 1950s anybody living on the west side of Athlone need never have crossed the town bridge as the shops of Connaught Street catered for their every need.

Busy at work on the telephone kiosk in St Mary's Place in the early 1960s are three unidentified staff members of the Dept of Posts & Telegraphs. However, the children in the foreground have been positively identified as Irene and Michael Heavey Jnr.

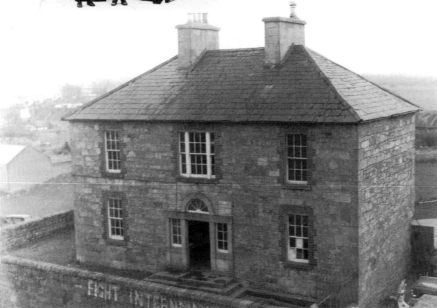

The Old Dispensary, St Mary's Place. This was one of the rare cut stone buildings of old Athlone. It was demolished in 1974 to make way for the building of Athlone Shopping Centre. The Dispensary was a dreary building internally but because it stood high above street-level it was a favourite spot for political rallies. In 1920 Larry Ginnell and Harry Boland addressed a public meeting from here, and watched in horror as the British military charged the crowd with fixed bayonets. It was also the scene of a major Blueshirt meeting in 1933.

In this classic and often reproduced photograph the Foys are pictured outside their family shops in Church Street. Donal Foy is driving and Michael Foy (affectionately known as 'Scorcher') is the back-seat passenger. It is interesting to note that in the shop windows a number of signs can be seen — one advertises an apparently Irish made bicycle, Lucania Cycles, while another notice reads 'Irish grown tobaccos'. Obviously Foy's were early advocates of a 'buy Irish' campaign!

Col Harry Rice, author of *Thanks for the Memory*, stood for the Dáil in 1957 as an independent candidate. His campaign was inspired by the appalling state of the Coosan Road. Another person who joined the campaign to improve the road was Cllr Paddy Hogan, who can be seen demonstrating to the local press that the only way two cars could pass on this road is if one of them is a toy car! The driver of the toy car was Tony Harkins of Ballyglass.

Portlick Castle on the shores of Lough Ree has a remarkable record. It has been lived in almost continuously since Norman times. Originally a Dillon castle, it stayed in the family possession until the late seventeenth century. After one short change of ownership it was taken over by the Smythe family in 1703 and remained their property until 1956. Over the past fifty years it has changed hands several times. The present structure is largely a fourteenth-century building with a fine Tudor block and some later but sympathetic additions. This photograph came from a Smythe family album.

This mock Gothic castle was designed by Richard Morrison as a gentleman's residence for William Handcock in 1814, shortly after his elevation to the peerage. It was the seat of the successive Lords Castlemaine for over a hundred years. In common with the homes of many Anglo-Irish landlords it became a target for anti-British feeling. On 3 July 1921 it was burned out as a reprisal for the burning of three houses in Coosan. The family never returned to the estate and it was subsequently divided by the Irish Land Commission.

Since the Shannon Navigation works of the 1840s the docks at Athlone have been a hive of industry. Today it is largely a residential area but in the past it boasted many local industries, including a distillery, sawmills, a woollen mill and a starch factory. In this view part of Lyster's Sawmills can be seen. The spire in the centre of the picture was on the Presbyterian Church which opened in 1860 — the converted premises now serves as a popular local restaurant, while the spire adorns a Catholic Church at Curry in Longford.

Church Street *circa* 1920. This summer scene shows many shops with awnings covering their signs, but the order of shops, as recalled by Frank Egan, was: Lipton's and Burgess & Co on the right; on the left the first premises is Campbell's bakery (complete with its doorway dated 1626), George Moore's hardware next door, followed by Paddy O'Neill's newsagency, Farrelly's undertakers, Parson's shoe-shop, Fetherstons (with the large tea-pot hanging above the door), Curley's, then the arch-way to Court Devenish, followed by Yeates grocery and wine & spirit merchants and Fleming's Medical Hall.

The end of an era for the docks! In this picture the old Weirside Mills, which had once been used by Farina Ltd as a starch factory, and had been built originally in the early nineteenth century as a distillery, come tumbling down to make way for new residential units. Local developer Noel Heavey made great use of this dockside site to bring new life back into the heart of old Athlone.

This view is taken from a photographic view album of Athlone, published by L. Hogan, Athlone, *circa* 1905. It shows a view of Church Street, where it was apparently safe to stroll in the middle of the road. Fleming's Medical Hall was run by James Fleming, who acted as a doctor to those who couldn't afford to visit one. In the aftermath of the sinking of the *Titanic* one Athlone family (Mrs Rice and her five young sons) was identified on the basis of a medicine bottle bearing the label of Fleming's Medical Hall.

In his classic pamphlet *Old Times in the Barony*, published in 1900, Fr John Conmee SJ, who was later to be made famous through his appearance in James Joyce's *Ulysses*, describes the joys of Market Day in Athlone: 'What a display of "dray" and "kish" and "crate" — those rustic argosies freighted with the simple merchandise of the homestead and the field.' Generations of farmers have brought their produce for sale to the Market Square in Athlone, created by the opening of the present bridge in 1844.

This quaint building, with its cut stone door-case, was St Peter's Loan Fund office in Excise Street. The photograph was taken around 1966. The premises was later demolished to make way for 'Áras Bríde' — the headquarters of the Athlone Meals on Wheels service.

This idyllic scene looking from Mardyke Street towards Church Street and the Bawn was engraved *circa* 1821. The sign on the right-hand side indicates The Sun Hotel (the forerunner of the modern Royal Hoey Hotel), which was opened by Thomas Kelly in 1803. The building in the centre of the picture appears to be a single-storey thatched premises — today it occupies the same site but has gained considerable height.

The Ranelagh Endowed School was opened in 1764 as a Protestant boys' school. In 1880 there were sixty-seven pupils: forty-eight borders and nineteen day boys. By 1936 numbers had dwindled to the point that it was no longer viable, and it was closed. The school had been a mainstay of education in Athlone, and had played a major role in the introduction of a number of sports to the town including rugby, soccer and cricket. The Ranelagh School complex was acquired by Gentex as a factory site. The school was demolished in 1991.

The new Post Office in Barrack Street opened its doors to the public on 4 September 1937, three weeks after a sub-office was opened in Mardyke Street. We have Kitty Kilkelly to thank for this view of the new Post Office without any other buildings around it. While one of the women appears to be posting a letter there is no sign designating the building as a post office nor are there footpaths along Barrack Street.

A hive of industry — the sorting office staff in Athlone Post Office, Barrack Street, in the late 1950s.

This photograph was taken in Pearse Street in 1961 before the demolition of two buildings, the old Bank of Ireland office and the Agent's House next door, to make way for the new Bank of Ireland branch office. The inscribed stone plaque over the fanlight of the house reads 'Paoli, Wilkes, Lucas and Liberty. R.S. 1770'. Paoli was a celebrated Corsican patriot. Lucas, from Dublin, and Wilkes, from London, were the civil rights reformers of their day. 'R.S.' stands for Robert Sherwood, an Athlone resident who died in 1786.

Despite this wintry scene complete with meagre Christmas lighting, Pearse Street in the 1950s was a thriving business street with a proliferation of smaller shops and some quality residential housing. Here doctors and solicitors had their offices and consultation rooms while the largest business was that of Lyster's builders' providers. The street was formerly known as King Street, having been so named in 1804 to honour King George III of England.

In the 1920s Athlone Woollen Mills was one of the leading manufacturers of pure wool tweeds and serges. This photograph, from one of their own promotional booklets, shows part of the worsted spinning department 'with all the most modern types of worsted spinning machinery'.

At work in Athlone Woollen Mills. The Mills were founded in 1859. This photograph, from a promotional booklet, *The Making of Athlone Tweeds and Serges*, dates from around 1920. It shows an employee working the swing-rake wool washer. In this early part of the process the wool was passed through the machine containing a scouring liquid which resulted in a thorough cleansing without damaging the natural fibres. The booklet boasts that the Mills 'are planned and lighted according to Twentieth Century ideas and fitted with machinery, the introduction of which has rendered all previous types obsolete ...'.

The town bridge was built as part of the Shannon Navigation Works of the 1840s, replacing the Elizabethan bridge which was by then hopelessly inadequate. As part of the contract seventy tons of metal castings arrived in Athlone in 1843 for the swivel arch on the Connaught side. In this, the only known photograph of the swivel span in the open position, it appears as if the occasion may be a military regatta around 1919.

The picture recalls the era of the temporary bailey bridge which was in place in the late 1950s and early 1960s while the new fixed span was being built. It was an exciting and sometimes frightening experience to cross it. One of the hazards of the wooden structure was that heavy vehicles were liable to break or displace the boards. Here traffic has come to a halt while emergency repairs are being carried out.

Apart from views of the Market, for some reason, views of the Connaught side of Athlone are far rarer than those of the Leinster side. In an album of views, published around 1905, Larry Hogan (of Church Street) featured this much-reproduced view of Connaught Street. On the left, beside the pillar-box and pump, is the premises of Mr Keane, victualler while across the street are Walsh's and Campbell's. The Walsh family have, without doubt, the longest surviving family business on the Connaught side of Athlone.

The first train to cross the Shannon to the West crossed over this viaduct on 21 July 1851 en-route to Galway. The train left Athlone at a quarter to four and arrived in Galway at twenty minutes to six. T.P. O'Connor once said of this bridge, designed by G.W. Hemans, that 'of all the prospects [he] had seen in Europe, the sight dearest to [him] was the graceful railway bridge over the Shannon at Athlone'.

This view of a deserted Market Square, with Athlone Barracks in the background, was most likely taken from the top of the Castle Keep *circa* 1898-99. Unfortunately it is very difficult to make out any detail on the shop-fronts on the left, except the name 'Central Hotel' painted between two windows at first-floor level. This was Geraghty's, which included a milliner's shop as well as a short-lived hotel. The premises was taken over by Dixon's around 1900. Many years later there was a Central Hotel in Custume Place.

Work in progress on the building of the new factory for Gentex in the 1930s. This picture was obviously taken in the summer as evidenced by the two haystacks, each with a bicycle parked against it. Above the building can be seen the cupola of the old Ranelagh School.

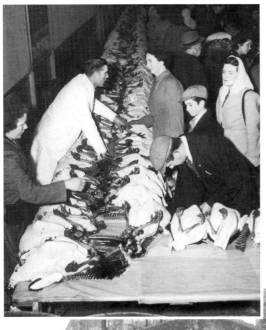

Here locals seek a bargain at one of the great turkey fairs in St Mary's Hall in the 1950s.

Fisheries is, perhaps, the oldest commercial activity in Athlone. The monks of the Cluniac monastery were trading in eels and salmon prior to the building of Athlone Castle in 1210. In 1293, Thomas de Pyckering, constable of the castle, accounted £4-16-0 for the sale of 3,600 eels. In the great Athlone tradition of selling fish beneath the castle walls, Fitzgerald Brothers of Connaught Street — with their mobile fish stall — were a regular feature in the Square in the 1960s.

2

Sport and Entertainment

Garrycastle Races was an important fixture in the local social calendar. Begun in 1848 as a one-day event, it developed into a two-day meeting. By 1863 it claimed to be second in importance to the Curragh Races. Apparently the races were abandoned in the 1860s after they became the scene of a serious faction fight. They were revived in 1894 and again in 1913 and held each year until 1924. Here the race committee are pictured on the steps of the stand in 1914.

'Oh yes she is!' 'Oh no she isn't!' This charming 'Dame' was none other than Charlie Byrne as he appeared in a pantomime in Athlone in 1976. Charlie, who was a stalwart of the All Ireland Drama Festival and Athlone Little Theatre, was an extremely talented amateur actor. For a number of years pantomimes with a local flavour were staged by the Athlone-born impresario Edward Farrell. This wonderfully mischievous study was captured by Charlie's fellow thespian Paddy Martin who kindly made it available to me.

This little band of musicians and entertainers came together as The Magpies in 1936 to help Fr. Pinkman raise the necessary funds for the conversion of the middle block of Athlone Workhouse to a parish hall. They included some of the brightest local talents of the day. BACK ROW: Mae Webb, Patsy Martin, A.J. Faulkner, Dermot Webb, Frank Illing and R. Leitch. FRONT ROW: Rita Milligan, Marie Lyster and Ruth Coen. Many of them later graced the stage of St Mary's Hall in dramas, musicals and concerts.

Athlone was famous for music and particularly for a fine piping tradition. One of the most famous local bands was the Athlone Clan Uisneach Pipers' Band. BACK ROW: Timmy Curley, Gilbert Hughes, Joe Scally, Jack Scally, Tom Keating, Jack Preston and Paddy Kearney. FRONT ROW: Pat Doran, Bobby Gallagher, Tommy Hunt, Dan Sullivan, Jack Sullivan and C. Miley. The banner was presented to the band by antiquarian and historian Francis Joseph Bigger.

This is a picture from a local fancy dress ball *circa* 1910, identified in the 1970s by Mrs Lily Molloy of Dublingate Street. She recognised seven of the participants: towards the right of the back row is John Doyle wearing a hat with a white band, with Batty Doyle as Santa Claus beside him; second in the next row is Eugene O'Flynn, with conical hat; the 'couple' beside him are Albie Wright and Dick Kilkelly; in front of them is Daisy Campbell in the dark dress, and slouched in front is Bob Campsie.

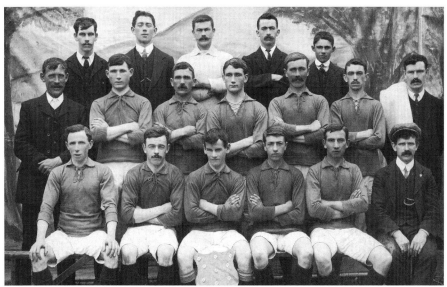

Athlone Town Football Club became affiliated to the Leinster Football Association in 1892, but the club had been founded in 1887. This Athlone team, St Patrick's League was one of two rival local teams in the 1911–12 season. BACK ROW: J. Allen, T. Kirby, Bill Downey (goalkeeper), P. Henry and P. 'Scratch' Flannery. MIDDLE ROW: J. Looby, Joe Monaghan, Terry Keegan, John Monaghan, Johnny Galvin, Mick Rafferty and W. Roper (trainer). FRONT ROW: Michael Hannon, Tommy Kilkenny, Michael Coyle, Jack McLoughlin, Joe O'Meara and Tom Donoghue.

The Athlone Town team of 1934–35. BACK ROW: Jack Finnerty, Paddy Scanlon, Tommy Farrell, John Henry, Jackie Downey. FRONT ROW: Mickey Hogan, Bill Barlow, Pa Dempsey, Johnny 'Pongo' Malynn (captain), Tommy 'Bullet' Brennan, Paddy 'Ruby' Barlow and Ivor Greally.

Celebrating fifty years of Athlone Little Theatre, at a reception in Athlone Rugby Club in 1986, were Larry Hanley, Marie Lyster, Shirley Whooley, Aileen Coughlan and Alfie Faulkner. Mrs Whooley was the daughter of Lt Col Michael Cosgrove, the founder of the theatre. The other four were the surviving founding members of the Little Theatre at the time of the Golden Jubilee, and all had given a lifetime of service to entertainment and culture in Athlone.

Attending the All Ireland Drama Festival in the Sportex Hall in 1955 were: Lennox Robinson (adjudicator), P.J. Lynott, Dan Doyle (Limerick), Shelah Richards (adjudicator), A.J. Faulkner, Mrs Doyle, P.J. Lenihan, Seán O'Beirne (Scariff), Ferdie Lee and Brendan O'Brien.

The Blue Crochets was one of the legendary dance bands of old Athlone. BACK ROW: Mick Daly, Maxie McLoughlin, Frankie O'Brien, Freddie Harvey. FRONT ROW: Jack Behan, Johnny O'Leary, Jackie Harvey, Jimmy Behan with singer Liam Fetherston at the microphone.

When local musician Barney Burke decided to emigrate to America the Athlone Jazz Maniacs decided to give him a grand send-off. LEFT TO RIGHT: Paddy Prendergast (drums), Paddy Kiely, Steve Croughan, Ben Gordon, Jimmy Behan, Evelyn Gordon (piano), Johnny Quinn (banjo) and Barney Burke (conductor).

At the launch of Tommy Gallagher's boat *Clorina* at Hodson Bay were: Tommy Gallagher, Canon John McCarthy, Derry McMahon, Cecil English, Syd Shine and local garda and river enthusiast Mick Mannion. Apart from having a lifetime's interest in boats and boating Tommy Gallagher of Castle Street was an expert on radio and TV, and is said to have built the first television set seen in Athlone.

Athlone Boat Club members pictured at Islandbridge, Dublin, having represented Connaught in the Inter-Provincial Championship 1950/51. Mr O'Toole (D.E. Williams), Willie Creavin, Joe Lacken, Maurice Geary (ESB), Harry Oliver (Mullingar), Liam Fetherstone, Cecil English, Martin Dolan, Jim Smith, Michael Hynes, Harry Duncan. In front is the cox, Brendan McFadden.

The cast of Athlone Little Theatre's production of *God's Gentry* in 1972, produced by Aileen Coughlan. BACK: Kevin Fahy. BACK ROW: Anne Flanagan, Paddy Martin, Mary Gahan, Owen O'Riordan, Regina Daly, Seán Masterson, Catherine Dolan, Joan Walsh and Harry Smith. MIDDLE ROW: Adrian Harrington and Peggy Sweeney. FRONT ROW: Frances Shanahan, Adrian Fortune, Pat Lillis, Joan Shanahan and Linda Higgins. Missing from photo: Liam Heavin.

Athlone's Ballroom of Romance was undoubtedly The Crescent, a ballroom built by the Shine family and attached to the family shop. In the 1960s 'Syd & the Saints' were known throughout the country and indeed in England. The line-up was: Brian Studdert (vocalist), Syd Shine (Hammond organ), Peter Keighery (lead guitar), Joe Flynn (bass guitar), Finbar O'Keeffe (rhythm guitar) and Frank Somers (drums).

Connaught Wanderers AFC 1906. This team took on a strong Dublin side, Reginald, winners of the Leinster Junior Cup in 1904–05, in a match at the Ranelagh pitch and won by four goals to one. Among the team was a very young future international, Dinny Hannon. BACK ROW: P. Galvin, J. Donoghue, J. Monaghan, J. Looby, M .Geoghegan, J. Galvin and J. Harwood. FRONT ROW: J. Smith, M. O'Meara, D. Hannon, M.J. Hannon and W. Monaghan.

Athlone Golf Club celebrated its centenary in 1992. This photograph of members of the Garrison Golf Club on the Batteries, taken in 1905 by Elliott & Fry, includes: BACK ROW: Miss Sryton, Joe Lyster, P.V.C. Murtagh, Louis Treacy, C.E. Fair, Tom Chapman, J. Vaughan and W. Briscoe. MIDDLE ROW: Florrie Ferrier, Emma Ferrier, Mrs Briscoe, Mary McCormack, Mrs Murtagh, Florrie Burgess and Kitty McCormack. IN FRONT: J.D. McCormack, Mona McCormack, Hilda Burgess and Peter Chapman. The youngest golfer in the photograph, J.D. McCormack, later became an Irish International.

Athlone Minors AFC 1927/28. This photograph was taken in Galway when the Athlone team beat a Galway team by ten goals to nil. BACK ROW: Mickey Hogan (trainer), Gerard Flanagan, Jack Finnerty, John Sweeney, Tommy Farrell, Mickey Moore, Dinny Hannon. MIDDLE ROW: Mike Broderick (refereee), Patrick Browne, Paddy 'Ruby' Barlow, Pa Dempsey, Jimmy Dempsey, Paddy Farrell, Joe Connor and Joe Scally (club secretary). IN FRONT is T. Manning.

Athlone Town AFC, Leinster Junior Cup winners 1921–22, pictured with some of their supporters. BACK ROW: Martin Farrelly, G. Hynds, Jim Sweeney Snr, T. Molloy and Peter O'Flynn. THIRD ROW: Tom Ghent, Danny Hanley, T. Browne, W.J. Bracken, Alan Smith, M. Naughton, F. Finneran, and John Greene (trainer). SECOND ROW: E. O'Flynn, M. Broderick, P. Colohan, J. Kennedy, John Sweeney, A. Enright and Joe Monaghan. FRONT ROW: Dinny Hannon, M Harkins, Frank Ghent, P. 'Scratch' Flannery, Jim Sweeney and Johnnie McManus. Missing from photo is team member Norman Lyster.

In the late 1960s it became obvious that one of the facilities which Athlone most lacked was a swimming pool. A committee was set up to further the aim of getting a swimming pool for Athlone and among those who lent their enthusiasm and support were: BACK ROW: Jimmy Spollen, Eamon Green, Michael Byrne, Chris Hunter, Fr Mark Mimnagh and Maj Gen M.J. Murphy. FRONT ROW: John Keenahan, J.D. Martin, Frank Fahy, Tom McKeown (builder, Ballinasloe), Jim Kearns and Brendan Manning.

For many years the Fair Green was a favourite stand for the circus when it visited the town. This view of Duffy's Circus, complete with its wooden trailers and big top, recalls the golden era of the Irish circus in the late 1950s. The photograph was taken by Dr Chapman of the *Westmeath Independent*, himself a keen amateur photographer. It shows the Fair Green with a hard concrete border and cattle pens.

Rugby has been played in Athlone since 1886. This team of 1935–36 were the legendary Shannon Buccaneers, twice winners of the Leinster Provincial Towns Cup. BACK ROW: D.F. McCarthy, P. Scanlon, A.C. Rynehart, J. Burrell, W.R. Williams, D. Davis and R.P. Hennessy (touch judge). MIDDLE ROW: J.P. Barrington, J.G. O'Connor, J.E. Cornish (captain), D. Murtagh and J. Mullen. FRONT ROW: W.R. Amos, P. Quinn, F.N. McDonald and P. Condron.

Athlone Town AFC has a long and illustrious history. The team pictured here were winners of the Blackthorn Trophy 1968-69. BACK ROW: Jackie Quinn (coach), P. Conway, Donal Crowley, Mick O'Brien (goalkeeper), J. Cleary, Jimmy Greene and Seán Gallagher (manager). FRONT ROW: C. Flanagan, Ray Bushe, P. McGrath, Mick Dalton, T. McCarthy and J. Joyce.

Of the second full musical performed by Athlone Musical Society in February 1908 the *Westmeath Independent* reported: 'Miss MacCormack was the recipient of two magnificent floral tributes to her splendid gifts as both an actress and singer ... and a pair of valuable bracelets from some unknown admirer. Other recipients of tributes were Miss Disney, Miss Foy, and Miss Murray. Mr Haywood received complimentary floral tributes as did Mr Aldwell. Miss Walker was accompanist and the delightful violin obligato was played by our talented town violinist Miss May Madden.'

The height of fashion. These followers of sport and fashion were captured on camera at the Athlone Open Tennis Tournament of 1903. The Garden Vale Tennis Club was a very popular club in the late nineteenth and early twentieth centuries.

The cast of *Dark is the Hour Before Dawn* presented by The Railwaymen's Progressive Club, at the Shannon Cinema in February 1926. BACK ROW: Paddy McNamara, Paddy Behan, Thomas Garland, Emily Geoghegan (Mrs McNamara), Jack Nally, Hannah McManus, Thomas McGuire, Edward Geoghegan, Gerard Murray, Anthony Shine (in uniform). THIRD ROW: John Hardiman, Thomas Molloy, P. Hughes. SECOND ROW: Thomas Shine, Joseph Donoghue, May Murray (Mrs Kilfeather), P. Sherlock, Josie Murray, Mick O'Neill, Maud Geoghegan, Michael Mullin, Eileen O'Brien. SEATED IN FRONT: Thomas Conlon and W. Curley.

This group were all members of St Peter's Badminton Club 1922–23. They are pictured outside St Peter's Church of Ireland off Pearse Street.

Three founder members of Athlone Sub Aqua Club recover a belaying pin from the cutter *Audax* in Portlick Bay in September 1973. Left to right: Robbie Walsh, Richard Looney and Richard Foy. The *Audax* was one of the last vessels to pass through the Ballinamore & Ballyconnell canal around 1860. The thirteen-ton *Audax* was owned by W.R. Potts of Athlone at that time. It later became the property of the Smythe's of Portlick and finally went to the bottom of Portlick Bay following ice damage in 1900.

The craft of boat-building has a long and distinguished history in Athlone. In 1797 James Curley was a boat-builder in Big Meadow. In the twentieth century several boat-building families were working along the Strand. These included Wards, Nortons and Brownes, with Keneaveys working at Dry Cow Island. Walter Levinge made the first Shannon One Design in 1921 and was still making them fifty years later. Here Walter Levinge of Creaghduff is putting the finishing touches to a Shannon One Design assisted by Ambrose Duggan.

A group of film enthusiasts pose for the camera outside the Ritz Cinema in Custume Place in April 1941. The occasion was a Midnight Matinee in aid of the NSPCC. The Ritz, built to the design of Michael Scott, had been opened the previous year. For over four decades it provided a haven of entertainment in the heart of Athlone, much of that time enjoying a healthy rivalry with the Adelphi Cinema in Garden Vale. The Ritz Cinema was demolished in 1999.

Big Top Productions, the brainchild of local impresario Edward Farrell, raised a great deal of money for local charities. Here members of the cast met Maureen Potter when she did a show in Athlone in the 1980s. BACK ROW: Doreen Byrne, Anne Colleran, Anne Casey, Eileen Jennings, Joan Larkin, and Camilla Brennan. MIDDLE ROW: Chrissie Healy, Edward Farrell, Maureen Potter, Karina Keogh and Myra Hogan. In front are Gael Kilduff and Olive Martin.

At Dublin Airport en route to Oslo, where 'The Town' were playing Valerengen FC in the second leg, first round, of the UEFA Cup, having beaten them three goals to one in St Mel's Park. ON THE STEPS, FROM TOP: Joe Healy, David Flynn, Eunan Blake, Eugene Davis, Noel Larkin, Mick O'Brien, Carl Humphries, Andy Stevenson, Kevin Smith. ON GROUND: Dougie Wood, John Minnock, Paul Martin, John Duffy (captain), Terry Daly, Amby Fogarty (manager), Padraig Nicholson, Cyril Barnicle, John Darnley, Eamon Kenny, Kieran Henson, Martin O'Gorman, Tommy Grenham, Christy Tighe, Tom O'Brien and Capt Kevin Fogarty (Aer Lingus).

Here local photographer Fergus Rowan, in a prize-winning photograph, captures the excitement as Shannon One Designs are rigging at the jetty of Lough Ree Yacht Club 1955.

This interesting collection of posters was photographed in the 1950s on the wall of the office of Athlone Printing Works. It shows the variety of entertainment to be had in Athlone. There are cinema posters for both The Ritz and The Adelphi, posters for shows in St Mary's Hall, Sportex Hall and The Church Hall, Ganly Place as well as one for a photographic exhibition in The Bon-Bon, and posters advertising a scheme for the insurance of Bulls, and another one for a dance in Ferbane.

3

Education and Religion

Dean John Crowe, St Peter's Parish, Athlone, pictured with his popular sacristan Tom Moore, admiring one of the new clocks for St Peter's Church before these were put in place in the 1950s. The clocks were presented to the church by Thomas Hughes, Coolagoriffe, Clonown. Dean Crowe, who was responsible for building SS Peter & Paul's, died in 1955. Today he is commemorated in the naming of the Dean Crowe Theatre, a state-of-the-art theatre housed in the building which once served as the parish church for St Peter's parish.

The laying of the foundation stone for the new Franciscan church, 22 January 1930. The three clergymen standing at the table are: Rev Philip Murphy OFM (Guardian Athlone Friary), Most Rev Dr James McNamee (Bishop of Ardagh & Clonmacnois) and Msgr Thomas Langan (Vicar General of the diocese). The altar-boy to the right of the pole is Billy Shine.

The laying of the foundation stone for the new church of SS Peter & Paul, 29 June 1932, excited considerable public interest. Officiating was Dr Edward Doorley, Bishop of Elphin. The work had commenced on the site in August 1930. On St Patrick's Day, 1937, following a solemn procession from the old church, the first mass and first baptism took place in the new church. The official opening of the church was held on 29 June that year, and exactly fifty years later the church was solemnly consecrated by Bishop Dominic Conway.

Marist Brothers School Choir 1926, winners of the Bishop's Cup for Plain Chant at the Longford Feis, and the Railwaymen's Cup for School Choirs at the Athlone Feis that year. BACK ROW: R. Reynolds, W. Byrne, W. Murray, S. Tuohy, S. Lyons and P. McManus. THIRD ROW: A. Kearney, P. Hanley, P. Kilroy, V. Kilroy, W. Martin, J. Mullins, J. Fallon and B. Dempsey. SECOND ROW: J. Spollen, D. Norton, Br John Mary (conductor) and P. Norton. FRONT ROW: D. Norton, R. Norton, P. Marsh and M. Judge.

Staff and pupils outside the Bower Infants' School, Fair Green, in the 1950s.

St Mary's Church of Ireland, Athlone. This church was built in 1827 but the tall, square bell-tower is a survivor from the earlier church of 1622. Mrs Goldsmith, wife of Dean Goldsmith (a cousin of the poet Oliver Goldsmith) is buried in this tower. The tower once had a steeple which can be seen in some earlier engravings of Athlone. In the church porch the mearing stone is preserved. It is a relic of the Elizabethan bridge of Athlone and once marked the boundary between Westmeath and Roscommon.

Farewell function for popular Church of Ireland rector, Rev Canon E.H. Langton May, to mark his retirement and departure from Athlone in 1981. LEFT TO RIGHT: Daphne Bigley, Mrs May, Tom Hunter, George Allen, Rev Langton May, June Nash and Eddie Griffin. Canon May had served as rector in St Mary's, Athlone since 1958. He retired to live in Kildare where he died in 1986.

St Peter's Brass Band, 1937, pictured outside the church. Included in the picture are: J. Sloyan, J. Behan, M. Flynn, E. Sloyan, J. Flynn, M. Galvin, L. Hanley, P. Hegarty, J. Behan, P. Dowling, E. Butler, J. Creavin, M. O'Connor (flag bearer), F. Carney (staff), E. McGee (flag bearer), T. Hanley, P. Lyons, L. Behan, P. Creavin, P. Behan, F. Madden, J. Butler, P. Kiely (leader), M. Prendergast, M. Woods, G. Wheatley and F. Duffy.

Work almost completed on the building of the Catholic church of SS Peter & Paul in 1936. The building, designed by Ralph Byrne, was built to hold approximately 1,000 people. It is a church of such large proportions that it is frequently mistaken for a cathedral. The twin towers, symbols of SS Peter & Paul, rise to 126 feet. Externally the church is finished in Portland stone and Irish granite. The stained-glass windows include work by the Harry Clarke Studios, Early & Co and Sarah Purser.

Church Unity Week, 1988. Pictured in the sacristy of St. Mary's Church were: Fr Frank Gray (Adm St Mary's Athlone), Bishop Walton Empey (Church of Ireland Bishop of Meath and Kildare), Bishop Colm O'Reilly (Bishop of Ardagh and Clonmacnois) and Canon Ivor Power (Rector St. Mary's Church of Ireland Church, Athlone).

An ecumenical group at St. Mary's during the visit of Cardinal Logue in 1905. BACK ROW: Mr McDermott-Hayes (*Westmeath Independent*), Michael Burke, Michael O'Meara and Mr Geoghegan (Coach Factory, third from right). MIDDLE ROW: Michael Kilkelly (second from left), James Coen, Dr Thomas Burgess, James Egan, Mr Geoghegan (Prince of Wales Hotel), Robert English. FRONT ROW: Dr Thomas Langan, Fr James O'Farrell, Cardinal Logue, Fr Michael Burke, Fr Conefrey and Fr Macken.

The old Garrow School at Retreat (above), which served as a school for Protestant girls from 1909 until the 1930s. It was later acquired by the Marist Order and greatly extended to become Our Lady's Hermitage in 1940. The Hermitage (below) became the novitiate for the Marist Brothers, attracting novices from England, Scotland and Ireland. The old Garrow building can still be detected on the left of the newer complex.

Pictured outside the church of SS Peter & Paul following his consecration as Bishop of Jos, Nigeria, is Most Rev Dr John Reddington SMA, with Most Rev Dr Browne, Bishop of Galway on his left and Most Rev Dr Lucey on his right.

This view of the church of SS Peter & Paul and the town bridge is one of the most hackneyed scenes of Athlone. Most local photographers have taken it at some time or another, possibly because it captures the essence of Athlone. Prior to the building of this church in the 1930s the most famous landmark was, it appears, the railway bridge.

Detail from the Kilroe monument in St Mary's R.C. church, Athlone. The marble monument by John Hogan Jnr depicts Fr Kieran Kilroe (1798–1865), parish priest of St Mary's, who was responsible for building the church. Contemporary accounts tell us that 'the likeness of Fr Kilroe has been most accurately caught'. The monument was erected in 1873.

The old Marist National School, St Mary's Place, which was completed in 1885, had among its early pupils John McCormack, who was to become a world famous tenor, and Michael J. Curley, the future Archbishop of Baltimore and Washington. The school served until a new school at Grace Park was opened in 1963. In 1978 after renovation it became St Ciaran's Hall, the meeting place of the Knights of St Columbanus.

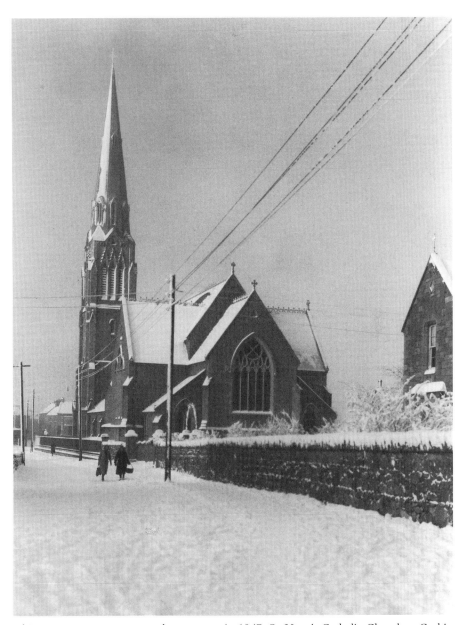

This snow scene was captured on camera in 1947. St Mary's Catholic Church, a Gothic church designed by John Bourke, was completed in 1862. The tower and spire, which is one of the landmarks of the town, is 180 feet high, surmounted by an ornamental cross. It is recorded that the person who first fixed the cross in position was a local man named Crawford. In 1905 the original cross was bent and the top stones of the spire shaken during a storm. The cross was replaced, as was the capstone of the spire.

The Sisters of La Sainte Union arrived in Athlone in 1884 and became involved in education, accepting both boarders and day pupils. The boarding school quickly established a reputation as one of the leading schools of its kind in the country. Its reputation can only have been enhanced by this promotional postcard from around 1950 showing girls availing of the sporting facilities in the school grounds.

A group of girls from the orphanage at Summerhill, run by the Sisters of Mercy, pictured at Athlone Railway Station before their annual outing in the 1950s.

At the official opening of Athlone Vocational School (now Athlone Community College) on 26 May 1978 were Seán Flood, John Wilson TD (Minister for Education), Seán O'Loughlin (CEO Westmeath Vocational Educational Committee) and Brendan O'Brien (Principal Athlone Vocational School).

This panoramic view of the Marist complex in St Mary's Place and Gleeson Street was taken during the 1960s when a firm of steeplejacks was called in to carry out some necessary repairs at St Mary's Church. Br Brian of the Marist Brothers, seizing the opportunity, gave his cameras to the workmen to take some 'aerial' views. In the foreground is the old National School, next door is the Intermediate or Secondary School and beyond that the Marist residence and outbuildings and the upper storey of the Athlone Printing Works.

Religious fervour in Athlone in 1918. This photograph, taken by Charlie Backhouse, shows a procession passing up Glasses Lane (now Griffith Street) and captures the religious fervour of the day. Mr Johnny O'Brien, a staff member of Athlone Printing Works, is the cross-bearer leading the young veiled communicants. Few photographs survive showing these old houses on the northern side of the street — today all is changed and there are modern houses on both sides of Griffith Street.

A sweepstake was organised by Dean Crowe as a fund-raiser for his new church. One of his previous draws was declared illegal, resulting in a court appearance for Dean Crowe in 1924. He still continued to promote draws and this one, his last, was made in March 1934. The spectators to the left of the drum included Nora Dempsey (née Moore), Mollie Keane, Helen Nolan, Guard Duffy and Jimmy Geoghegan. To the right of the drum are Dean Crowe, John Grenham, Joe Huban and J. Rice, the manager of the National Bank. The blind-folded schoolgirls are not identified.

This photograph, from a Broderick family album, is believed to show the solemn procession from the old St Peter's in Chapel Street to the new church of SS Peter & Paul, on 17 March 1937. The procession is leaving O'Connell Street and proceeding down Pearse Street.

The Friary Choir, 1928. BACK ROW INCLUDES: Pat Sherlock, Con Lee (third left), Barney Hayes and Richard Norton. FOURTH ROW INCLUDES: Sonny Kearney, Kieran Norton, Johnny Menton, Paddy Scanlon. THIRD ROW INCLUDES: Joe Scally, Agnes Hoey (third left), Patsy Lane, Maura Daly, Molly Carty and Timmy Curley. SECOND ROW INCLUDES: Annie Cunniffe, Mabel Tallon (third left), Fr Philip OFM, Fr Aidan OFM, Peg Flannery, Annie Kearney, Mary Roe and Bridie Ross. FRONT ROW INCLUDES: Nancy Norton (second left), Agnes Kearney (fifth left), Maisie Gough (second right) and Kathleen Egan. The photographer was Charlie Backhouse.

The shell of an unfinished seventeenth-century Franciscan Abbey on Abbey Road, together with the graveyard which served Athlone until its closure in 1871. The last burial in the Abbey was in 1948, over seventy years after its official closure.

This view of St Mary's Catholic Church shows the pre-Vatican II arrangement, with the high-altar, altar rails and pulpit. The pulpit, which was octagonal in shape, was designed by J.J. McCarthy of Dublin and executed by James Pearse, Brunswick St, Dublin; the latter was the father of the patriot brothers Pádraic and Willie Pearse. The pulpit was removed in 1974. This photograph was taken during a Gregorian chant festival in the late 1950s.

Bishop Kirby, the newly consecrated bishop of Clonfert, is presented with a picture of his old national school, The Dean Kelly Memorial School, on the occasion of his visit to the school in 1988. Larry Fagan (NT Principal), Bishop John Kirby, Paula Gibson NT and Canon Patrick Murray PP (St Peter's, Athlone).

Football stars in the Dean Kelly National School in 1974. BACK ROW: Larry Fagan NT, Terry O'Neill, Seamus Donoghue, Brendan Cauldwell, Martin Gilligan, Ken Benson, Kieran McConnell, John Egan, Frank Nolan and Gabriel Curley. FRONT ROW: Brendan Conaire, Pádraig Brennan, Declan Fitzgerald, P.J. McCormack, Liam Tone, Paul Egan, Seamus Hughes, Tony Duffy, Dermot Browne and Seán Hunt.

Gaelic League class from circa 1920. BACK ROW INCLUDES: J. Martin (Athlone Printing Works, first right). MIDDLE ROW INCLUDES: J. Bradley (second left), Frank Fitzpatrick NT (fourth left), Bro Charles (sixth left), T. O'Brien NT, Liam Rabbette, E. Doran. FRONT ROW INCLUDES: Maud Milligan (second left), Mrs P. Murtagh, Peter O'Farrell, Fr Goodwin, Adm St Mary's, P.V.C. Murtagh, Mrs J. Martin, John O'Brien and Bro Bonaventure.

4

Shops and Shopkeepers

This imposing business at the junction of Connaught Street and King Street was founded by John Grenham in 1911. One of the great entrepreneurs of old Athlone, Grenham established a thriving and multi-faceted business with a bar, grocery and travel agency. The award-winning travel agency still survives ninety years later and is run by his granddaughters, trading from the same premises. During its first year in business it sold passage-tickets for the ill-fated *Titanic* voyage of 1912. This picture captures some of the lively bustle of Connaught Street in the late 1930s.

Ms Monica Coghlan outside the family pub in Irishtown. After Coghlan's time the premises was acquired by the Cloonans, who ran the pub next door. This ornate shop-front has changed very little in over fifty years. Today the premises is a private house.

One of my favourite shops during my childhood was Lipton's in Custume Place, under the management of Kevin Connolly. The attraction for a child was the endless tins of loose biscuits, with their glass lids. Lipton Ltd was one of the major grocers and provision merchants in the town and traded here until they moved to a larger supermarket premises in Church Street in 1968. This photograph, from the late Kitty Kilkelly's album, was taken around 1940 but the shop remained unchanged for many years.

Geoghegan's in Mardyke Street was a well-known newsagency and stationers which survived until the 1960s. At the time this photograph was taken in the 1930s it was run by Kitty Farrell, who had married Michael Geoghegan of the Coach Factory, and she was trading under her married name. It had previously been a grocery shop run by Ned Farrell. The shop was acquired by Whitelaw's in the late 1970s and was rebuilt. They traded in curtains and blinds until the shop was taken over by Kilroy's, who deal in electrical goods.

James Egan's bar and grocery occupied a pivotal position at the junction of Dublingate Street and Mardyke Street. This photograph, taken around 1940, shows James's widow Maria Egan on the left chatting to a customer, Miss Kitty Kilkelly. Maria was affectionately known as 'The Little Flower'. She died not long after this picture was taken and the bar was taken over by Bernard Egan, a nephew of her husband. In the late 1940s Billy Case, the proprietor of Case's Supply Stores in Dublingate Street, took over this premises which he ran as a general hardware store.

The Webster family were in business in Athlone since at least the 1920s. Mr Webster managed the Athlone branch of Dillon's, the Galway Jewellery firm which specialised in Claddagh Rings. He later took over the premises and traded successfully until the 1950s when he sold to Aidan Ward, who opened a very popular shoe shop which traded here for almost fifty years. Today Louis Walsh and family run a shop here called 'Treasures' which stocks a fine array of antiques and collectibles.

Wooden kegs of Beamish XXX Stout delivered outside Murray's at the corner of King Street and Queen Street in the 1920s. The barman outside the door was Martin Naughton, a long-serving employee of the firm.

Butler's of the Square with shop-hands Joe Tell (of Irishtown) and Mary Walsh.

The removal of the shop-front from the Medical Hall at 37 Church Street, which was run by James O'Brien until his retirement in 1959. For a time he also had another branch in Connaught Street where the Misses Galvin ran a newsagency in later years. The building workers are James Byrne, Terry Whelan, Dessie Byrne and Mattie Grehan. **Below:** The new-look 'Claffey's' in 1959. Peter Claffey bought the premises from James O'Brien and opened his 'House of Bacon', a general grocery concern specialising in farm produce including bacon, eggs and country butter.

This rare photograph was taken by the late Kitty Kilkelly. It is of the Cox's Imperial Hotel in Gleeson Street. Here James Cox ran a small high-class hotel in a building leased from the Marist Brothers. When the lease expired in the 1930s it was not renewed and the hotel closed. The Marist Brothers extended by adding a third storey and also by adding a three-bay block at the Garden Vale end of the building. It then became the residence of the Marist Brothers. It is called 'Champagnat House' after the founder of the Marist order.

The Royal Hoey Hotel in Mardyke Street in the 1940s. There has been a hotel on this site for over two hundred years. In the early twentieth century it was Claxton's Hotel and it later passed on to Jimmy Hoey. He acquired two small shops next door and incorporated them into his newly renovated premises. The Royal has a long tradition as a family-run hotel. Notice the steps up to the entrance door and the shield on the wall stating that the 'GSR Motor Bus Stops Here'.

Originally this was Poole's Garage in Irishtown. Mr Poole had a cycle shop in Custume Place before getting involved in the motor trade with the arrival of the car. This photograph shows the premises as Blackledge's Garage, complete with its petrol pumps. The posters read 'Petrol Quick Service — No Waiting — Electric Pumps'. A mechanic attends to the car while Miss Kitty Kilkelly faces the camera. Blackledge's was later taken over by Gills. The premises was demolished in 1974 to provide access to Athlone Shopping Centre from Irishtown.

In the 1930s the Prince of Wales Hotel, Church Street, was Athlone's leading hotel. It was a family-owned establishment run by Michael Geoghegan and family. One of his daughters, Lillian, was the first wife of Col Harry Rice while another daughter, Moira, managed the hotel until her death in the late 1950s. In the early 1960s the wing of the hotel which contained the shop-front was knocked to make way for a car-park. It was extensively refurbished and rebuilt. It was taken over in 2000 and has recently been demolished.

Christy Bigley (right), plumber and hydraulic and sanitary engineer, prepares to move out a newly made boiler from his premises in Irishtown. This photograph was taken in the late 1950s. Two firms, Bigley and Campsie, dominated the plumbing trade in the town for many years. A walk through town will still reveal man-hole covers, hydrant covers and assorted iron-ware bearing the names of these well-known local craftsmen.

This bar and grocery, located at the junction of Mardyke Street and Glasses Lane (now Griffith Street), was owned by the Geoghegan family who ran the Prince of Wales Hotel. In the early twentieth century it was Tom Carty's. Unfortunately we do not know the identity of any of those standing in the doorway, though one presumes them to be members of the Geoghegan family. The advertisements at the tops of the windows are for 'Van Houten's Cocoa', 'Martell's Three Star Brandy' and 'Hennessy's Fine Old Brandies'.

Hayden's in Irishtown was a popular grocery shop run for many years by John Joe Hayden, a native of Carrick-on-Shannon. John Joe came to Athlone as a young man and, according to Frank Egan, worked in Yeates in Church Street before setting up on his own. Here the proprietor is seen chatting to Kitty Kilkelly.

The staff of Thomas Burgess & Son outside the shop in Church Street, *circa* 1910. Few Athlone businesses can boast such a long and distinguished history. Thomas Burgess bought the stock-in-trade of local draper Matthew Headen in 1839 and the business has flourished ever since. Thomas Burgess & Son became a private limited company in 1910. In the early 1950s it was taken over by Ian Boles of Boyle but still happily trades as Burgess & Son Ltd.

The Sweeny family were closely associated with the business life of Athlone for almost a century. This was their first shop, situated in Mardyke Street, in a premises which stood where Connell's stands today. The photograph shows the proprietor holding his child's hand as they stand on the steps outside. We know very little about this shop other than that it sold delph and furnishings. Note the birdcage hanging above the entrance door.

This old photograph shows a rare view of Macken's drapery shop at No 14 Church Street, possibly taken prior to 1900. This family-run business had started here around 1880 but there had been a drapery shop on the site since at least 1837. The last of the family in business here was Kevin Macken, who sold to Bert Heaton. Mr Heaton had also acquired Coyle's Cellar Bar next door and demolished the two buildings to build a larger shop before transferring his business from across the street.

Celebrating thirty years in business in 1928 Richard Wheatley, hairdresser, his family and staff pose outside the shop in Pearse Street. Left to right: Miss Wheatley, Mr Sullivan, Richard Wheatley and his son Joe; the fifth person, who is blurred, was a Mr Maxwell. The Wheatley family celebrated a century in the hairdressing business in Athlone in 1998. Joe Wheatley opened a salon in Northgate Street in 1944 which is still carried on by sons Richard and Pearse.

This 1940s' view of 10,12 & 14 Custume Place shows Denis O'Halloran's hardware store. O'Halloran had been a partner in Byrne & O'Halloran in the Square until he acquired this premises from Robert Moore in 1939. Next door was Boushell's newsagent and tobacconist, (formerly O'Neill's). It was later taken over by Josie Egan. Next door to this was Farrelly's Undertakers, a family business run by brothers Paddy, Martin and Jack Farrelly.

The awning says it all. This is James Browne, late of Custume Place, standing outside his shop in the early 1940s. He had taken over from Mr Acheson in Mardyke Street in the early 1930s and converted the shop from a newsagency to a chemist's. In his spare time James Browne shared the family enthusiasm for boating. When he retired in the late 1940s the business was taken over by Frank Rouse. The premises has now become part of Connell's gift shop.

Proud publican Stephen Kelly Snr outside his bar in Mardyke Street in 1980. This photograph was one of a number taken by P.J. Murray for Frank Egan's book *Bridging the Gap: Athlone's Golden Mile 1920-1980*. Stephen Kelly was a native of Moore and at that time held the record for the longest serving shopkeeper or publican in the town of Athlone.

5

Events and Occasions

This dramatic view of the bridge of Athlone captures the excitement of the day, Tuesday 28 February 1922, when the military barracks was taken over by the Free State Army under the command of Comdt General Seán MacEoin. Many of the young men here assembled were probably hoping to join the fledgling Irish army.

The reviewing party on the Fair Green for the inspection of the Midland Volunteers in December 1914: John Sheehan (reporter, the *Westmeath Independent*), Owen J. Dolan, Col Maurice Moore, Sgt Major Brooder, Thomas Shine (sixth from left), Geoffrey O'Donoghue, Thomas Moore and Edward Costello (holding a bugle).

The funeral of Thomas Hughes, Bogganfin, making its way up Northgate Street from the Town Hall in October 1924. Hughes was one of five young Republicans executed in Athlone Barracks by the Free State Army on 20 January 1923. The others were Michael Walsh, Hubert Collins, Stephen Joyce and Martin Burke, all natives of Co Galway.

When the legendary Lord Mayor of Dublin, Alfie Byrne, came to the opening of SS Peter & Paul's in the 1930s his presence caused quite a stir. Among those who queued up for his autograph was Rosaleen Flanagan (later Rosaleen Naughton). Byrne also performed the unveiling of a plaque on the birthplace of T.P. O'Connor in Castle Street as the two had served together in the House of Commons.

Members of the McCormack and Foley families in Athlone for the launching of the joint Irish and American issue postage stamps commemorating the centenary of the birth of John Count McCormack on 6 June 1984. Back row: Cyril Count McCormack and his son John McCormack. In front: Dorothy Foley, Carol Ann McCormack, Johanna Kelly, Patricia Tinne and Grace Foley with young Louise Tinne standing in front of Dorothy Foley.

This German engraving purports to be a view of Athlone in 1691. It is similar to a number of Dutch engravings which were used by the Williamites as an early form of war propaganda. Other contemporary prints depict Derry and Enniskillen. While it may not bear any close resemblance to Athlone, scenes similar to the combat scene in the foreground were witnessed here during the sieges of 1690 and 1691.

In December 1914 Col Maurice Moore of Moore Hall reviewed the Irish Volunteers in the Fair Green. Col Moore, who was a veteran of the Connaught Rangers and had served in the Kaffir, Zulu and Boer Wars, was an instructor for the Irish Volunteers. His presence in Athlone for this display of strength excited great public interest as is evidenced by the massive turnout. The sign on the right of the picture refers to Ferrier's, a large supplier of agricultural supplies and farm machinery who had their showrooms in the building later used to house the Garden Vale Cinema.

New recruits parading on the barrack square, Custume Barracks, in 1922 prior to the issuing of uniforms.

The *Westmeath Independent* was founded by James Martin in 1846. Over a century later the then managing director, Dr T.P. Chapman, revolutionised the production of the newspaper when he acquired a rotary press from the *News of the World*. In this picture Dr Chapman can be seen commissioning the new press in October 1953 — it continued to serve faithfully for more than thirty years.

Cutting the ribbon to mark the official opening of the new offices of the *Westmeath Independent* in Sean Costello Street in October 1991. Cllr John Butler (Chairman Athlone UDC), Margaret Grennan (editor), Mary O'Rourke TD (Minister for Education), Mr Nicholas Nally (editor, the *Westmeath Examiner* and Chairman of the Board of Directors for the *Westmeath Independent*), Martin Nally (MD *Westmeath Independent*), and Jimmy Spollen (former editor).

This scene of industrial devastation recalls one of the greatest catastrophes to befall Athlone in the twentieth century. On the night of 11 November 1940 the extensive premises of Athlone Woollen Mills was destroyed in an accidental fire, putting 500 people out of work. In order to prevent the fire from causing even greater devastation the army was called in to carry out controlled explosions in Northgate Street. Both the Roslevin School and the Longworth Hall were blown up and the spread of fire was curtailed.

Athlone Fire Brigade staff taking delivery of their first fire tender, pictured on Abbey Road in 1946. BACK ROW (standing on tender): F. McLoughlin, J. Mannion, J. Earley, P. McLoughlin. FRONT ROW: H. Troute (driver), W. Reid (captain), T. Stewart, J. Kirby (Fire Chief), M. Downey, J. Shanks, P. Stewart (sub-officer).

Pictured at the opening of the John McCormack exhibition in the Prince of Wales Hotel in September 1963 were: Mrs MacEoin, Gen Seán MacEoin TD, Maura Mullen, Michael Heavey, Ernan Morris and Michael Martin. The Exhibition ran for two weeks and engendered a considerable amount of local interest in the life and times of the Athlone-born tenor John Count McCormack. General Seán MacEoin was a personal friend of John Count McCormack.

Pictured at the opening of the Oliver Goldsmith Exhibition in Athlone in 1966 are Seamus O'Connor (County Librarian, Longford-Westmeath Joint Library Committee), N.W. English, Celine Butler (Librarian, Mullingar), A.J. Faulkner, Ernan Morris (Librarian, Athlone), Canon John McCarthy (St Peter's, Athlone), Mrs Lily Allen and Mr Brendan O'Brien.

A group of uniformed soldiers of the IRA from Beggar's Bush Barracks in Dublin and from Longford Barracks, and a few local men who had already received their uniforms, assembled in St Mary's Place in preparation for the takeover of the barracks. We know from published accounts that this photograph was taken at half past ten on the morning of Tuesday 28 February 1922 and that the officer commanding the troops was Comdt General P. Morrissey.

The funeral of Brigadier-General George Adamson was one of the largest gatherings of its kind ever seen in Athlone. George Adamson, a native of Moate, was closely associated with the take-over of the barracks in February 1922. Less than two months later, on Monday 25 April, Adamson was shot dead in Irishtown. The bullet, fired by a fellow-Irishman, was one of the first shots in the Civil War. George Adamson was buried in Mount Temple churchyard.

At the launch in Athlone Library of *After Doomsday*, a poetry book by Conleth Ellis, on Ash Wednesday 1982 were: Dr Joseph Cassidy (Bishop of Clonfert) who performed the launch, Conleth Ellis (poet and chairman of *Poetry Ireland*), Gearóid O'Brien (librarian), Maria Mahon, Leo Mahon, Bernie Mahon, Dermot Bolger (publisher with Raven Press), Niall Mahon and Cllr Padraic Dunne (chairman Athlone UDC). Conleth Ellis, a native of Carlow, lived and taught in Athlone until his sudden death in May 1998. He has left a major legacy in terms of his published poetry in both English and Irish.

Turning on the Christmas lights has long been an important event in the local calendar. In this picture, taken about 1957, the Church Street Traders were gathered to mark the occasion. BACK ROW: Jack Foy, Seamus Fox, Bert Heaton, Paddy Hogan, Bob Poynton and Billy Keogh. FRONT ROW: Angela Farrell, Mary O'Brien, Edna Shaw, Mrs Webster, Mrs Grant and in front master Rodney Shaw.

When President Patrick Hillery visited Athlone August 1981 he was afforded a civic reception by Athlone UDC. BACK ROW: Cllrs John Keenahan, Des Lynch, Jimmy Lennon, Padraic Dunne, and Cieran Temple. FRONT ROW: Cllrs Mary O'Rourke, Sean Fallon (chairman), President Hillery, Ciaran McGrath (Town Clerk) and Mr Brian Colgan (Westmeath County Council).

The opening of the new Telephone Exchange in Barrack Street in 1959. J.W. Devlin (PO Engineer), M.G. McGeeney (Westmeath County Manager), P.M. Morgan (District Engineer), T. Mannion PC, T. Fahy PC, P.J. Hamill (Telephone Traffic Department), P. Killion PC (Glasson), M. Nearney (County Engineer, Roscommon), J. Telford MD (Athlone Woollen Mills) and Erskine Childers TD (Minister for Posts & Telegraphs).

Members of Athlone UDC pictured with Cllr Sean Fallon in 1979 when he received his chain of office as Council Chairman. BACK ROW: Des Lynch, John Keenahan, Jimmy Crehan, Cieran Temple. FRONT ROW: George Allen, Sean Fallon, Norrie Egan (Acting Town Clerk), Frank Waters and Paddy Hogan.

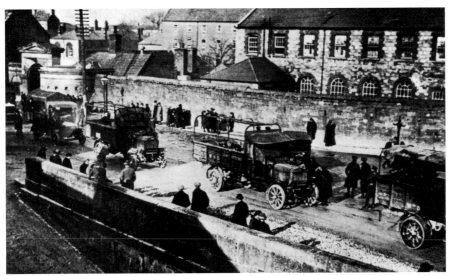

On the morning of Tuesday 28 February 1922 a convoy of British army vehicles left Athlone Barracks en route to the Curragh. We are told that from six o'clock that morning the troops were leaving in small detachments. By seven o'clock 120 motor vehicles laden with troops and equipment had passed through the town. At eleven o'clock Col Hare of the British Brigade Staff met the in-coming Irish military personnel and formally handed over the Barracks to Comdt Gen Seán MacEoin.

Crowds gather at Parson's Corner to view the destruction in Northgate Street following the accidental burning of Athlone Woollen Mills in November 1940. The building on the left was The Central Hotel, a temperance hotel run by the Misses Roden. Above the Genoa Café, at first floor level, can be seen the sign for Emily Gill who traded here as a hairdresser until 1943.

Presidential visits are always a proud moment in the life of a town. Here President Mary Robinson is greeted by a shy young admirer bearing a posy of flowers. The President was in Athlone to open the fortieth All Ireland Drama Festival in May 1992. The young girl making the presentation is Carey O'Brien, a granddaughter of Brendan O'Brien who was Festival Director from 1953 until his death in February 1992.

An exhibition to mark the centenary of the birth of John Count McCormack was held in Athlone Library in 1984. Pictured were: Tom Egan (Connaught St), Mrs Mary O'Rourke, TD, Cllr Cieran Temple (Chairman Athlone UDC), Kathleen Egan and Desmond Egan poet and writer who performed the opening of the exhibition.

At the launch of the Journal of the Old Athlone Society in 1975 were: A.J. Faulkner, President OAS, N.W. (Billy) English (Hon Secretary and Hon Editor), Julia Begley (council member) and Mr Ernan Morris (Hon Treasurer), OAS. Both Billy English and Ernan Morris did major work in assembling archives of old photographs in Athlone. The Old Athlone Society, through their museum and archives, preserve all sorts of ephemera as well as artefacts relating to the town.

Visit of Cardinal John D'Alton, Archbishop of Armagh and Primate of All Ireland to Athlone on 7 July, 1957. This picture was taken in the grounds of the Bower Convent. The priest with the microphone is Fr Patrick Bennett CC, Dr J.J. Keane (in dress suit), standing behind the Cardinal is Fr Philip McGivney (Adm St Mary's) and to the right of the Cardinal is Bishop McNamee.

The floods of 1954 were the benchmark by which twentieth-century flooding was measured in the Shannon basin around Athlone. In the picture **above** Miss Nellie Hughes of Bunnaribba, Clonown is helped from her house by two local guards, Thomas and William Gallagher. Bringing up the rear the man with the beret is John Healy, a journalist with the *Irish Times*, and the gentleman behind is Dr J.J. Keane. **Below** A group of local children, whose names have unfortunately not been recorded, look quite pleased at the opportunity to pose for the camera.

Unloading the last cargo arriving in Athlone by barge around 1955. The delivery was a new Intertype Composing Machine for Athlone Printing Works. To witness this historic event were: Paul Chapman, Joe Cunningham and John Glennon, all of the *Westmeath Independent*, Walter Levinge, Dr Norman Furlong and Rosemary Furlong. The gentleman at the right wearing the cap is Col H.J. Rice, author of *Thanks for the Memory*. Unfortunately nobody thought to record the names of the dock workers.

Recalling the glory days of steam: Loco No 719 at the Midland Great Western Station in Athlone around 1960. This station served as the main passenger station for Athlone from its opening in 1851 until it closed in January 1985.

The commemoration of the Tercentenary of the Siege of Athlone was one of the most significant events in modern times in Athlone. Pictured at the reception in Athlone Castle on New Year's Day 1991 were: Patrick Cooney MEP, Mary O'Rourke, TD (Minister for Education) and Albert Reynolds, TD (Minister for Finance).

The laying of the foundation stone for St Kieran's Terrace. This was the first housing scheme undertaken by Athlone UDC in 1905. On the left the gentleman with the stick is Mr Baille, the principal of the Ranelagh School, in the centre (with trowel) is Michael Hughes, Chairman Athlone UDC and to the right is Joseph Concannon, Coosan, the builder. The houses were built at a cost of £150 each.

Repairs in progress on the Weir Wall in 1934. A portion of the Weir Wall had given way overnight. Locals reported hearing a loud crash and in the morning a fifteen-foot breach was found in the wall. It was successfully repaired without any detrimental effects on the production of electricity at Ardnacrusha.

Agricultural shows have long been a favourite attraction in Athlone. In more recent times they have been held in the Showgrounds at Deerpark Road but here we see a show in full flight in the Fair Green. In the foreground the hard-stand has been divided into sections for trade displays. In the middle-ground the large canopied stand houses competition entries, including home-produce, arts and crafts while in the background a gymkana is in progress.

Opening of the Garda Barracks in Barrack Street, BACK ROW: Gardaí John Golden, David Minogue, Thomas Gallagher, Pat Connor, Maurice Tobin, John Banim, Matthew Moran, William O'Connell, Charles Molloy, Frank Fahy and Pat Hyland. MIDDLE ROW: Mrs Maxwell, Shiel, Minogue, Gallagher (W.J.), Carey, Tobin, Banim, Hoyne, O'Connell, Molloy, Fahy, Hyland and Golden. FRONT ROW: Det Officer Frank Maguire, Fr M. Brennan, Gda Pat Carey, Sgt J. Lynch, Fr Valentine OFM, Canon W. Quinn, Supt J. Devine, Dean Crowe, Fr Tully, Sgt P. Shiel, Gda R Maxwell, William J. Gallagher and Edward Hoyne.

Two serious local fires of the 1960s. **Above:** Peter Claffey's 'Snacks' in Church Street is burnt out. He later rebuilt it and opened the first pet shop in Athlone, 'The Ark'. It is now Bridie McNeill's flower shop. Next door was Moran's butcher's shop. **Below:** Michael Coyle's butcher's shop in Pearse Street is destroyed by fire. Next door was J.P. Newell's chemist shop. Mr Newell, an avid bird-fancier, kept an aviary and many of his prize birds perished in this fire.

An important day in the cultural and social life of the town when Cllr John Butler (Chairman Athlone UDC), and Mme Martine Buron (Mayor of Chateaubriant), in France are pictured at the formal signing of the charter of twinning for our two towns, on St Patrick's Day 1995.

During the war years the workers in Gentex saved turf on the bogs around Athlone to fuel the factory boilers. In this picture a newly patented turf-cutting machine, devised by Gentex staff, is launched. Mr Killian, from Glasson, Chippy Sommerville, Michael O'Connor, Billy Beville, Seán Lemass and Mr Duckworth admire the new contraption.

A group of young Athlone scouts prepare to attend the Eucharistic Congress in Dublin in 1932. BACK ROW: Frank Egan (flag bearer), Paddy Quinn, Jackie Behan, Master Lane, Frank Martin, Peter Egan, Master Behan, Peter Marsh, Richie Murray, Stephen Lyons and Isodore Timon. SECOND ROW: Brian Macken, John Bracken (assistant scout master), Commissioner John Stokes, Ballinasloe (on loan to Athlone), William McCrea (chairman of scout committee), Gerry McEntee (assistant scout master) and Niall Casey. FRONT ROW: Sean Flannery, Master Verdon, Andy Kearney, Desmond O'Brien, Eamon Hanley, Joe Fallon, Donal Flanagan and Pearse O'Carroll.

6

People and Personalities

This beautiful group photograph of John Count McCormack with his family was taken during one of his visits to Athlone in 1908. He is pictured outside his parent's house at 5 Auburn Terrace. Left to right: Andrew and Hannah (née Watson), John with his son Cyril in arms and his wife Lily (née Foley), herself a noted soprano. Judging by the quality of the picture the photographer was, most likely, G.V. Simmons.

This historic photograph of the first committee of the Midland Volunteers was taken by G.V. Simmons in 1913. The movement was started at the instigation of Mr McDermott-Hayes, the editor of the *Westmeath Independent* and the committee were, BACK ROW: Peter O'Brien, Alfred Warby, Sean O. Mullany (Jack Mullany) and Patsy Downey. FRONT ROW: Michael Curley, James Gough and Patrick Croughan.

The Chapman family pictured outside Garden Vale House (now Cooney's Pharmacy). The people standing to the left of the doorway are Thomas Chapman and his sister, in the doorway is Thomas's wife Elly (née Smith) while a nanny looks after master Ivan Chapman who is seated on the trap. Thomas Chapman was the proprietor of the *Westmeath Independent* from 1883 until his death in 1922 when he was succeeded firstly by his son Ivan (until his death in 1936) and then by another son, Dr T.P. Chapman, until 1970.

This photograph taken on the Promenade in Athlone in 1970 shows Kitty Kilkelly, Cyril Count McCormack and Gerald Dowling. Count McCormack was in Athlone to unveil the fine bronze bust of his father, John Count McCormack, by the Cork sculptor Seamus Murphy. With him are the two local people who did most to keep McCormack's memory alive in Athlone. Kitty Kilkelly raised the finances to employ Seamus Murphy to sculpt the bust and Gerald Dowling arranged for many important pieces of McCormack memorabilia to go on display in Athlone Castle Museum.

Visit of Joe Frazier, World Heavyweight Boxing Champion, to Athlone in 1974. Here Frazier is interviewed by Jimmy Spollen of the *Westmeath Independent* under the watchful eye of popular local waiter Michael Hynds. Famous boxers were no strangers to Athlone — John L. Sullivan, Jake Kilraine and Paul Pender all visited Athlone in search of their local roots. The most notorious Athlone-born boxer was the bareknuckle fighter Joe Elliott, whose career ended when he was shot dead by a sheriff.

When Princess Grace (Grace Kelly) was travelling with her young family to the West of Ireland to meet her relations in June 1961 she broke her journey in Athlone. The family stayed in The Shamrock Lodge Hotel. **Above** Princess Grace entering the Hotel after a stroll in the grounds. **Below** the family prepare to leave. These photographs were taken by local girl Angela Dunning (née Meares) who was a photographer with the *Westmeath Independent*.

This genial old couple Ralph and Maria Jameson (née Fallon) were photographed in the haggard at their farm in Ardnaglug, Cartrontroy, in 1928. It is believed that the photograph was taken by Fr William Sweeney (1896–1958). Ralph was nearly ninety when he died in 1929, Maria died in 1931 in her ninety-first year. This wonderful couple were the great-grandparents of the present Jameson, Marsh and Conway families in Athlone.

Jubilant in their old age; this group had good reason to smile for the camera. They were among the first to register for the 'Old Age Pension' in Athlone in 1908. Sadly we don't have a record of their names or dates of birth but these hardy individuals were claiming to be over seventy years of age — in other words as children they had survived the Famine, had witnessed the Shannon navigation works of the 1840s and the founding of Athlone Woollen Mills. They are pictured here outside Athlone Workhouse in Northgate Street.

This dashing young volunteer was Sean O. Mullany (or Jack Mullany), a native of the Strand. As an apprentice in Athlone Printing Works in 1913 he came under the influence of Mr McDermott-Hayes, the editor of the *Westmeath Independent*. Mullany was among the founding members of the Midland Volunteers, a movement which pre-dated the founding of the Irish Volunteers. His brief account of the founding of that movement was published in 1963. This rare photograph is one of the best visual records we have of the uniform worn by the Midland Volunteer force.

Visit of the famous nationalist politician and land agitator, John Dillon (1851–1927), to Athlone. This group was photographed outside the Prince of Wales Hotel. BACK ROW INCLUDES: John P. Hayden (second left), Mr Yates, D.J. Kelly (sixth left), P.V.C. Murtagh, P.J. Geraghty, T.C. Bannon and P. Hughes. FRONT ROW INCLUDES: John Dillon, V Rev Dean J.J. Kelly (St Peter's). The third figure seated is unidentified.

John Broderick, a native of Connaught Street and a member of a well-known bakery family, made his name as a novelist and critic. He was born in Athlone in 1924. He published twelve novels, a number of which also appeared in French translation. He died in Bath in 1989. In 1999 Athlone UDC named a new street, linking Sean Costello Street with Golden Island, in his honour. This photograph was taken by local photographer P.J. Murray before Broderick's departure for Bath in 1981.

This electioneering photograph of Frank Waters recalls one of the most colourful characters in public life in Athlone in the twentieth century. He was three times chairman of Athlone UDC, in 1952, 1962 and 1964. When a monster was reported to have been sighted in Lough Ree he immediately saw the value of such a sighting to the local economy and said 'Any Athlonians who do not believe in the monster should have their heads examined and if then found to be of rational mind, they should be deported.'

'Twisters Gang' was the name given to those working in the twisting department in Athlone Woollen Mills. This group, photographed in 1939, includes, back row: Paddy Browne, Mattie Marsh, J.J. Blake, Vincent Mack, John Verdon and Frank Lee. Second row: Christy Carroll, Peter Marsh, P.J. Lynch, Maurice Gough, Steve Marsh and Christy Reilly. In front: Sonny Gaffey and M. Coughlan.

This is perhaps one of the most famous photographs of a local triumvirate, each of them distinguished in his own right. The picture was taken in Custume Barracks in the 1920s and shows: John Count McCormack, Archbishop Michael J. Curley of Baltimore and Washington and Comdt General Seán MacEoin. Archbishop Curley was a native of Golden Island and Seán MacEoin was the officer who took-over control of Athlone Barracks from the British army in 1922.

A group of Athlone members of the Ancient Order of Hibernians (AOH) pose for posterity outside the old Friary. BACK ROW: Mr Gilmore, Mr J. Henry, Mr E. Farrell, Mr Watson, Mr Doyle and Mr Fitzpatrick. FRONT ROW INCLUDES: Mr J. Carroll (second left), Mr H. Rafferty (fourth left), Mr T. Berry, Mr J. Fahey and Mr Bigley.

A group of locals pictured in Coosan in 1916. BACK ROW: T.J. Mulvihill, Harry Waters, Bill Concannon with his daughter Maura (Mrs Fox) in arms, Peter Mulvihill, Kitty Concannon, Andrew Heavey, Maud Mulvihill (Mrs Mitchell), Jack Mullaney with Lily Concannon (Mrs Sleator) in arms, Nan Mulvihill (Mrs Crampton) and Brian Mulvihill. FRONT ROW: Matt Mulvihill, Lily Mulvihill (Mrs Jones), Larry Benson, Lisa Mulvihill with Mary Mitchell in arms and Martin Mulvihill.

The first St Mary's Hall Committee 1936. BACK ROW: Charlie Devine, Fr William Quinn CC (St Mary's), Tom Burke. MIDDLE ROW: Denis O'Halloran, Timmy O'Brien, John Reid, Bernard Heavey, William McCrea, Hugh Hanley and Fr John Pinkman (Adm St Mary's). FRONT ROW: Frank Macken, Frank Flanagan, P.J. O'Connor and Michael Martin. By the time this photograph was taken William McCrea had died; the photographer left a space for him in the middle row and inserted his head and shoulders from a family photograph.

Garret FitzGerald, leader of Fine Gael, with his wife Joan in Athlone in 1981 to support the cause of Sen Patrick Cooney (right) in his bid to regain a Dáil seat. Paddy Cooney who had been Minister for Justice from 1973-77 had spent the intervening years as leader of the opposition in the Seanad. In 1981 he made a successful comeback to the Dáil and was appointed as Minister for Transport and Minister for Posts and Telegraphs in the Fine Gael – Labour Coalition.

Members of Athlone Chamber of Commerce pictured with their newly elected chairman, Billy Walsh. BACK ROW: Arthur O'Riordan, Michael Lucitt, George Sheffield, Kerry Sloan, Cieran Temple, John O'Gorman, Egbert Moran and David Fenton, FRONT ROW: Fergus McCarrick, George Eaton, Billy Walsh, Seamus Ruddy and Jim Keane.

With his sartorial elegance and charm Harry Broderick, a tailor from Athlone, became the first local TD to take a seat in Dáil Éireann. He was elected as a Labour Party candidate in June 1927 but by Autumn that Dáil had been dissolved. He was re-elected to the new Dáil and served until 1932. He opened a tailoring establishment in Chapel Street in 1933. After twenty five years in public life, having served as TD, Urban Councillor and County Councillor, Harry Broderick bowed out of public life in September 1950. In less than twelve months he was dead.

Pictured at the opening of the Jubilee Nurse's Home (Dr Dobbs), Northgate Street: BACK ROW: W. Walsh (second left), P.V.C. Murtagh, Mrs Milligan (fifth left), Nurse Marrinan (seventh left), F. Flanagan, Mrs Chapman. MIDDLE ROW: Hon. Mrs Duncan, Mrs Telford, Mrs Hynes (seventh left), Mrs Geoghegan (Prince of Wales Hotel), Mrs Gladys Moore, Miss McGann, Rev Given. FRONT ROW: Lord Castlemaine, Mr Fleming, Mrs Murtagh (fourth left), Dean Crowe (sixth left), Mrs Milligan.

Pictured at a gala at Hodson Bay following the unveiling of a plaque commemorating TP O'Connor's birthplace in Castle Street, Athlone in 1936. The platform party includes: R. Kelly, Dr Vincent Delany (third left), Mr Molloy (Clonmacnoise), Mr Huban, Alfie Byrne (Lord Mayor of Dublin), Miss K.M. Kilkelly, Mr John Grenham, J.J. Lynch (first right).

Members of Athlone ICA plant trees on the Promenade in the early 1960s. LEFT TO RIGHT: Nuala O'Brien, Mollie Young, Olive Naylor, Kitty Higgins, Kay Geraghty, Mary Ryan, and Nano Nolan. IN FRONT: Angela Tormey and Nora Phelan.

The Dog's Home, Northgate Street, 1909. BACK ROW: T. Conlon, Mr Coffey, P. Flynn, Mr Coffey, E. Flynn, Mr Potter, Mr Brown and Mr Carroll. SECOND ROW INCLUDES: D. Cahalane, Mr Galvin (fourth left), Mr Daly (sixth left), Mr Dolan, M. Molloy, J. Fahy and son, Mr Bradley (manager of Athlone Gas Works). THIRD ROW: Mr Potter, Mr Muldoon, Mr Sheffield, Mr Flynn, Mr Campsie, Mr Bolger, O.J. Dolan, M.H. Foy, J. Coyle. FRONT ROW INCLUDES: Mr Topps, Mr Timon, Mr Macken, Mr Buckley, Mr Murray, J. Pilkington.

Bishop John Kilduff of Ardagh and Clonmacnois (1820–1867) was a native of Bushfield, Athlone. His diary for 1867 showed his plans for 'visitations' to twenty-two parishes. He began on St Patrick's Day and by 11 June had completed seventeen. By mid-June the over-worked bishop had fallen victim to typhoid fever. He died on 21 June and was buried in the crypt of St Mel's Cathedral. A popular and much loved pastor, it is estimated that his funeral was attended by no fewer than twenty thousand people.

Proclaiming the news. Local printer and entrepreneur Cieran Temple announces the launching of his newspaper the *Athlone News* in December 1961. Among those reading the posters are Paddy Ryan and Aidan Butler.

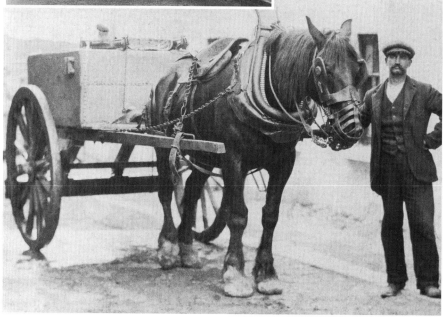

J. Dowling, pictured here leading his horse and cart, was a welcome sight on the streets of Athlone in the 1920s. Before the era of tarred roads our streets were glorified dirt tracks repaired by shovelling stone chippings into pot holes. Dust from these roads was a major problem for householders. The local authority employed Mr Dowling, with his watering cart, to patrol the streets of the town during the summer sprinkling them with water.

This is Eileen Kelly (née Smith) photographed beside the old pump in Chapel Street in July 1930.

Presidents all. A group of past-presidents of the Athlone guild of the ICA pictured with visitors from the Westmeath Federation and the National Council of the association. BACK ROW: Kitty Higgins, Angela Coyle, Nancy Kearney, Nancy Ball, Lily Allen, Maureen Rooney, Kay Garvey and Bridie Flynn. SECOND ROW: Mary Leech, Margaret Erraught, Una Flynn, Eilish O'Dalaigh, Mary O'Brien, Josie O'Connell and Nuala Hunt. IN FRONT: Nuala O'Brien, Julia O'Donoghue and Julia Hogan.

Seán Costello, a native of Cornamagh, was a Second-Lieutenant of F Company, Irish Volunteers. He had acted as a pall-bearer at the funeral of O'Donovan Rossa and heard Pádraic Pearse give the grave-side oration. On the Wednesday of Easter Week, 1916, the bloodiest day of the rebellion, he was sent on dispatch duty to Boland's Mill. In the aftermath of the fighting his body was found among the dead. In 1935 part of Irishtown was renamed Seán Costello Street in his memory.

Athlone Fire Brigade was founded in 1939. In 1980 four members of the service were honoured at a function in Athlone Town Hall, each having given forty years of loyal service. Here they are pictured with local fire chiefs: Eugene Fayne (Second Fire Officer), on the left and Seamus Hunt (Chief Fire Officer), on the right. The four firemen are: Patrick Grennan, Seamus Earley, Patrick Stewart and Frank McLoughlin.

Athlone ICA guild with their president May Dockery. FROM BACK: Margaret Macken, Lily Allen & Kay Geraghty, Mae Walker, Angela Coyle, Kitty Francis, Nuala O'Brien, Pauline Harrington, Teresa Keaney and Kathleen Ward. Mrs Connaughton, Joan Carty, Nancy Kearney and Maura Campbell. Mrs Travers, Margaret Erraught, Maura Longworth, Mrs Lackey, Rita Kenny and Mrs Doyle. Ruth Griffin, Nora Greene, Mrs Nicholson, Mairead Loughman, Jean Hamill, Doreen Quirke and Eileen Egan. Teresa O'Flaherty, Mary Leech, Mrs Cunniffe, Julia O'Donoghue, May Dockery, Mrs Bailey, Una Duffy and Gladys McElroy. SEATED: Lily MacCormack, Katie Flynn, Gretta Baird, Mollie Young and Mary O'Brien.

Charlie Backhouse on his island in the 1950s where he lived on a beached houseboat. Charlie Backhouse arrived in Athlone around 1905 and found employment in the Athlone Printing Works. He was also a gifted photographer with a studio in Irishtown. It seems that he 'inherited' the island, now known as 'Charlie's Island' but then known as 'Dead Man's Island', from another eccentric, a Mr Cummins, a reporter with the local paper who lost his job in the mid 1930s. Charlie died in February 1961 at the age of 89.

This fine study of an early Westmeath registered car 'LI 444' and its driver, shows Thomas Chapman of Garden Vale House looking relaxed behind the wheel. Chapman was a fearless nationalist; he campaigned for land reform, supported Parnell and in the aftermath of the 1916 Rising campaigned for the release of 'political prisoners'. In 1920 his printing works was burned down by the Black & Tans who took exception to the tone of some articles in the *Westmeath Independent*.

John Fahy, Athlone, one of the last skippers of the Shannon Development Company steamers which went out of service in 1914, with the Captain of the *St Brendan* passenger vessel on its arrival at Athlone docks in 1955.

Athlone Round Table — Past Chairmen (1965–1986). BACK ROW: Desmond Hogan, Paschal O'Gorman, Patrick Dolan, Malachi Cullen, Jimmy Reid, Derek McVeigh, M.J. Moran, Bernard Gill, Billy Maynard, Derry O'Dowd and Joe Lyster. FRONT ROW: Don Beddy, George Sheffield, Christy Reid, Anton Shevlin, Richard Flynn, Patrick Cooney and Paddy Reid. Missing from photograph were: Michael Carroll, Jim Patterson and Sean McGorisk.

During a break in the filming of an RTÉ television drama based on the German spies in Ireland during World War II, Comdt Jim Power (left) speaks to ex-spy Gunther Shutz. Shutz was among a group of spies interned in Athlone Barracks while Jim Power was among his gaolers.

Members of Athlone Camera Club (mid 1960s). BACK ROW INCLUDES: Paddy Coughlan, Paul Quast (third left), Joe McEntaggert and Brendan O'Brien. IN FRONT: Mary Rafferty (née Bannon), Bina Deery, John Harrington and Josie Bannon.

Staff outside the Midland Great Western Railway Station. BACK ROW: J. Fagan, Mr Conroy, B. Potter, H. Kerrigan, W. Campbell, J. Behan, Mr Butler, P. Murphy, T. Austin, W. Barnes (third right), P. Hanley and M. Harkins. MIDDLE ROW: T. Kelly, K. Warrington (fourth left), P. O'Rourke (second right) and Nano Fagan. FRONT ROW: J. Brennan, P. Bartley (third left), J. Earls, B. Kennedy, Mr Milton, P. Connell, T. Conlon and seated in front M. Hardiman.

Presentation to Brian Gormley, Town Clerk, on his departure from Athlone in 1974. BACK ROW: John Hardiman, Paddy Stewart, James J. 'Sonny' Gallagher, Seamus Bleakley, Ernan Morris, Cllr Tom Darcy, Cllr Jimmy Crehan, Cllr Des Lynch, Mr Joe Murphy (Town Engineer), Sean Lucy, Noel Heavey (architect), Cllr John Keenahan, Cllr Cieran Temple, Liam Ledwith, Aidan Gallagher, Martin Egan (solicitor). FRONT ROW: Frank Egan, Mary Tiernan (née O'Sullivan), Norrie Egan, Cllr George Allen (Chairman, Athlone UDC), Brian Gormley, Mrs Gormley, Cllr Mary O'Rourke, Mary McGee (née Connaughton) and Eugene Lee.

Those were the days! This debonair young man, pictured with his bicycle in 1908, is Gus Hynds, who ran a popular bar and lounge in Mardyke Street until he retired in the 1930s. He is seen here wearing a single-breasted, three-piece, tweed suit with matching cap. It would be nice to think that his clothes were made by a local tailor from tweed made in the Athlone Woollen Mills. The premises formerly run by Gus Hynds was later run by the Garry Brothers and has been run, since the 1940s, by James Moran of Irishtown.